New ideas with Embroidery on Paper

Erica Fortgens

D0562582

This book is a compilation of the following publications:

Borduren op papier met kraaltjes en embossing
2001 La Rivière creative publishers, Baarn, The Netherlands
ISBN 90 384 1580 X
Photography: Hennie Raaymakers, St. Michielsgestel
Photography styling: Willemien Mommersteeg, St. Michielsgestel
Illustrations: Erica Fortgens

Figuren borduren op papier
2003 Tirion Uitgevers, Baarn
ISBN 90 213 3351 1
Photography: Hennie Raaymakers, St. Michielsgestel
Photography styling: Willemien Mommersteeg, St. Michielsgestel
Illustrations: Erica Fortgens

Patchwork wenskaarten met borduren op papier
2004 Tirion Uitgevers, Baarn
ISBN 90 213 3435 6
Photography: Hennie Raaymakers, St. Michielsgestel
Photography styling: Willemien Mommersteeg, St. Michielsgestel
Illustrations: Erica Fortgens

Ecstasy Crafts
PO Box 525
Watertown, NY
13601 USA

Ecstasy Crafts
630 Shannonville Rd
Shannonville, ON
KOK 3AO Canada

Toll free 888-288-7131
Fax 613-968-7876
Email: info@ecstasycrafts.com
Website: www.ecstasycrafts.com

© 2004 Tirion Uitgevers bv, Baarn

ISBN 90 213 3464 X

Cover: Hans Britsemmer, Kudelstaart
Translation and DTP: Studio Imago, Amersfoort

This book is published by
Uitgeverij Cantecleer
Postbus 309
3740 AH Baarn
The Netherlands

Cantecleer is part of the Tirion Publishers bv

New ideas with Embroidery on Paper

Contents

7	Materials used
8	General method
15	**Embroidery on paper with beads and embossing**
16	Introduction
17	Cream-coloured cards with stylish gold
21	Flowers with golden leaves
24	Embossed parchment paper
28	Embroidery on paper with beads and embossing
32	Grey and pearls
36	Warm yellow with beads
41	Embossed parchment with cut-outs
46	Behind beaded 'bars'
50	Embossing with embroidered borders
55	**Figures embroidery on paper**
57	Introduction
58	Sunny Mandalas
63	Creations in light blue
69	Rosettes
74	Radiant stars
80	Pretty in pink
82	Floral designs in pastel green
86	Circles in purple
89	Elegant in aqua
92	Photos to frame and take away
98	**Patchwork greeting cards with embroidery on paper**
99	Introduction
100	Paperpatch paper
101	Green/blue Paperpatch
106	Golden Star
110	Roses
114	Composition in blue
118	Patchwork in green
122	Patchwork with embossing
126	Patchwork with L'ouvre
130	L'ouvre
134	Composition in gold

Materials used

- Very fine Erica® piercing tool with accompanying embroidery needle.
- Fine Erica® piercing tool with accompanying embroidery needle.
- Coarse Erica® piercing tool with accompanying embroidery needle.
- Erica® embossing tools in three different sizes.
- Erica® hobby knife
- Erica® cutting ruler
- Erica® piercing pad
- Erica® square cards (ideal for embossing)
- Erica® rectangular cards (ideal for embossing)
- Erica®'s parchment paper for embossing (for embroidery; also ideal for embossing – no light box needed!)
- A variety of multi-functional stencils are used to help with cutting and embossing, and different piercing patterns are included for elegant piercing and embroidery.
- The square stencils: Decorative, Elegant, Geometrical and Romantic, Allure, Antique and Starlight.
- The rectangular stencils: Passe-partout, Flower and Heart, Victorian, Ornament, Jugendstil, Bethlehem and Party.
- Embossing light box
- Small piece of soap
- Cutting pad
- Double-sided adhesive film
- Glue stick
- Cellotape
- Thread: Sewing machine embroidery thread weight #40. Recommended: Alcazar, Metallic and Reflecta, from Coats. Floss may also be used.
- Square embossing stencils (with many different borders): Decorative, Elegant, Geometric and Romantic
- Erica®'s embossing parchment, available in white, ivory, light blue, mint and pink
- Embossing light box
- Embossing tools in various thicknesses

Romantic EF 8002

Ornamental EF 8008

Geometric EF 8001

Passe-partout EF 8005

Flowers and hearts EF 8007

Elegant EF 8003

Decorative EF 8004

Victorian EF 8006

Antique EF 8009

Allure EF 8010

Classic EF 8016

Bethlehem EF 8014

Prima EF 8015

Party EF 8011

Starlight EF 8012

Jugendstil EF 8013

Multifunctional
ruler EF 0011

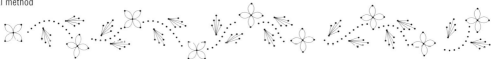

General method

Techniques

The best order to use in this combination of techniques is pierce, emboss, embroider, attach beads and finish.
Fold card open and place on piercing pad with front side up.

Pierce all dots carefully with very fine piercing tool. Hold the piercing tool as straight as possible so that clear holes are made. See photo 1.

Pierce the larger dots with the coarse piercing tool, making a large hole for multiple threads.

If you make a mistake while piercing the holes, place a small piece of cellotape on the back of the card covering incorrect holes and continue piercing.

Before removing the pattern from the card, hold both up against the light to ensure that all holes in the pattern have been pierced.

TIP
Keep the photocopies in a folder after use; if you have pierced them well you can use them again and again!

Photo 1

Photo 2

The needle

The needle must always be thinner than the piercing tool; use the needle that comes with the piercing tool.

> **TIP**
> Does your thread become frayed? Rub a very small drop of glue onto the end of the thread; it will dry immediately and keep the thread intact.

Embroidery

Work step-by-step following the instructionss for each individual card. Take one strand of thread about 30 inches or 70 cm long or if double thread is desired about 3 feet or 1.30 m. Thread the needle (use needle threader) and pull through until double thread is obtained. Insert needle through pierced hole from the back at the starting point. Leave about ½ inch or 2 cm of thread and attach to the back of the card using a small piece of cellotape. See photo 2. Do not cover pierced holes! Follow instructionss for each pattern.

> **TIP**
> How to use a needle threader: place the pointed wire tip through the eye of the needle. Now place the single strand of thread through the wire of the needle threader. See photo 3. While holding the needle in one hand, pull the needle threader (hold the wire firmly) and thread back through the eye of the needle. See photo 4.

Photo 3

Photo 4

Stem stitch

Insert the needle from the back at hole 1
and pull thread to hole 2 where needle is
put down through the hole. Go along the
back to hole 3 and pull thread to hole 4.
Go along the back to hole 5 and pull
thread to hole 6. And so on as indicated in
the diagram skipping two holes on the
front each time and one hole on the back.
For small curves skip one hole.

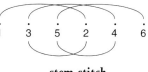

stem stitch

Important: Remember to come up on the inside of the curve. Pull
away the previous thread with your thumb, in order not to pierce the
previous stitch.

TIP

Use sewing machine embroidery thread. This thread is strong and
has a lovely sheen. Use a double thread. Note: never use a double
thread of Metallic, as this will make it extremely untidy. To create a
good finish you can also use a double thread of floss.

TIP

To separate floss: Cut thread to 70 inches or 1.30 m. To separate
one strand pull apart the strand a distance, then place the longer
end between your knees and hold gently. Holding the one strand
in your right hand and the 5 strands in your left, separate the
strands by keeping the thread taut and pulling up on the thread
allowing it to slip between your knees until fully separated.

TIP

To avoid knotting of the thread: Pull thread trough the card gently
and not too quickly. If the thread becomes twisted while working
with double threads, let the thread hang down with the needle so
it can unravel itself.

TIP

Make sure that the holes that have to be pierced large are in fact
large enough; a number of threads may have to pass through them.
If a hole does not turn out to be large enough while you
embroidery, pierce it again with the coarse piercing tool.

TIP

When embroidery on Erica®'s Parchment Paper, make sure that you stick the thread on the back as close as possible to the pattern, as the thread will shine through the paper. The best thing to do is stick it tight with a drop of glue (do not make a mess!) on an embroidered section, or weave the thread with the needle back through the stitches already made.

Embossing

Embossing constitutes an important part of this book; there are now 14 different multi-functional Erica® stencils available: see materials. Each stencil is uniquely designed with many patterns woven into the stencil that allow it to be used for many different sized designs using various parts of the stencil. It is the art of leaving out; just pick your choice!

Always make sure that you pierce first, then apply the embossing and then start embroidering: if you embroider first, you cannot emboss any more because of the tape on the back of the card.

Pierce pattern into the card

Choose the stencil that you wish to use and place it on light box, taping it down using cellotape.

Switch on the light. Place your card FRONT SIDE DOWN on top of the stencil and tape it to the light box.

First use coarse embossing tool to exert light pressure on the paper going to the edges of the stencil, later on use a finer one.

The paper will be raised on the front side of your project according to the stencil used.

Other applications with the stencils

The embossing stencils are also very suitable for stencilling: for this purpose you use a small ink-pad. Cover the rims which you do not use with cellotape.

Trace the borders with a gel pen; this is very effectual on, for instance, dark cards which you cannot emboss.

If you want to emboss on a dark card all the same, you proceed as follows. Place the cards between two identical stencils. Make sure that the stencils fit well when glueing them. Apply the embossing.

11

TIP
If you use card stock, you will need a light box.
If you use Erica®'s parchment paper for embossing (heavy duty parchment paper), you will not need a light box since the paper is transparent.

TIP
When applying embossing you can rub in the back of the card with a little bar of soap; this makes embossing much lighter and easier!

TIP
The following stencils are ideal to cut with: Geometric, Passe-partout, Allure, Antique, Starlight. Glue the stencil firmly to the card and make any desired cut out. Cut along the opening of the stencil or draw a fine pencil line and then cut. Please note: always cut along the same side of the opening in the stencil: this means that you have to turn the card with the stencil on it over and over again. This yields the best results. Use cutting pad and Erica®'s Hobby knife.

Figures
Use the stem stitch for the figures.

Beads
Many of the cards in this book are finished with beads. Important: Pierce the design onto the card, emboss your chosen design and attach the beads last; after the beads are on, you will not be able to emboss the card.
Use transparent thread; it is somewhat elastic and is good for fixing the bead. It's also nice to use a fine golden thread when you use transparent beads; the bead gives the gold extra shine!

Border at the top of these pages
Embroider the stems using stem stitch. For the leaves, Insert needle at the front through large hole. Draw the thread to the points indicated and insert needle. Flowers: use lazy daisy stitch (below).

Lazy Daisy stitch
Insert needle at front through hole #1. Push needle back through #1

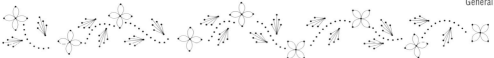

leaving a loop of thread on front of design. The loop should be large enough to reach hole #2. Push needle from back through hole #2, passing through loop on the front and insert needle back through hole #2 to secure the loop. Pull the thread so that the loop lies flat. The drawing shows the different ways of using this stitch in the embroidery designs for different and wonderful effects! The first loop should not be so tight that it loses its shape, but not too slack. Practice with the thread you are using to get a feel for it.

Finishing off

Fold the embroidered card and the cover sheet in half.

Using a glue stick, attach the cover sheet to the back of the card to cover the threads from the embroidery. Glue the cover sheet only to the side where there are threads to cover.

A message or greeting may be placed on the loose back half of the cover sheet.

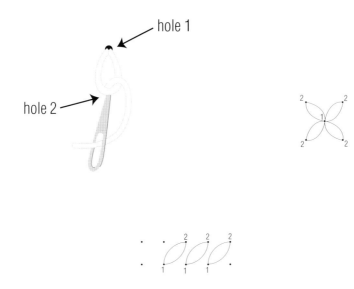

hole 1

hole 2

Mandala EF 8017

Circle EF 8018

December EF 8019

Merry Christmas EF 8020

Embroidery on paper with beads and embossing

Introduction

Embroidery on paper is on the move!

There are even more new techniques to combine! To start with, there are four new and wonderful embossing stencils. They're ideal to use, because now entire borders are on the stencil – no more endless moving the design along the edge! Each of the stencils has its own character. Their names are Decorative, Geometric (fun for men too!), Elegant and Romantic. What's nice about these stencils is that not only can they be combined with each other, but also you can choose from among the different borders on the stencil. Combine with an embroidered border and the possibilities are endless! You can use the stencils for cut-outs, or use other materials like relief paint. Or stencil with a paint-dipped sponge to make a pretty decoration on a card. The new Erica® parchment paper is a joy to work with; parchment paper lends itself beautifully to embossing. Used as the cover for a card (use a piece of cord to secure it) with a cut-out framing an embroidered bottom card, it is quite an innovation! And if you cut in the top card the embossed parchment paper can be used as a bottom card. It looks gorgeous combined with an embroidered border! And how about adding some beads? They are the rage right now; the look is lovely and elegant!

I hope you like this innovative twist on embroidery on paper; I know I very much enjoyed working on this book. Have fun!

Erica Fortgens

Many thanks to Leonie Heuyerjans, as well as Anneke Kaufman. Willemien Mommersteeg, thanks for all the tips!

Cream-coloured cards with stylish gold

See photo pg. 19

The Decorative embossing stencil is used for all these cards. Pierce the pattern in the card first and then use the indicated border, or make your own creation!

A1

Pierce the large hole in the centre using the coarse piercing tool. Draw the thread from this hole to the surrounding smaller holes as indicated. Sew on the beads.

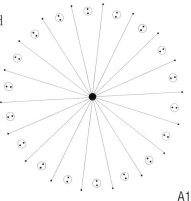

A1

A2

Draw all threads as indicated; sew on the beads.

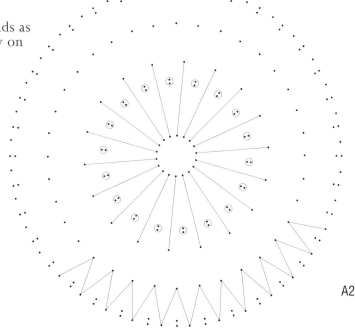

A2

17

New ideas with Embroidery on Paper

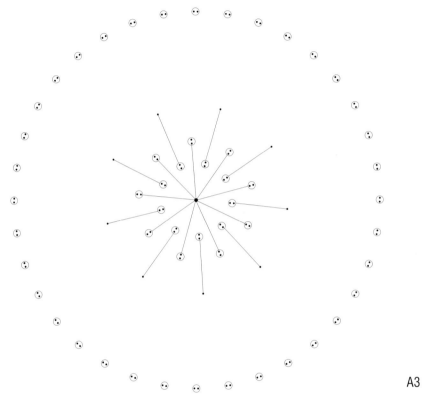

A3

A3
See instructions for A2.

Instructions on pg. 17

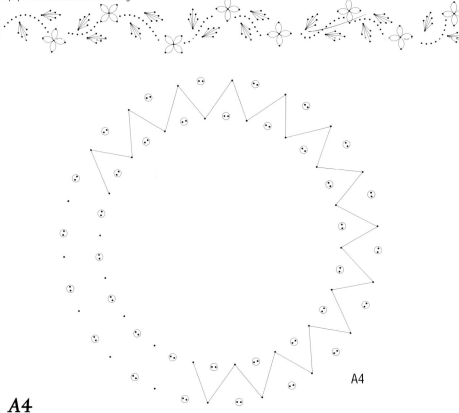

A4
See instructions for A2.

A4

A5
See instructions for A2.

A5

Flowers with golden leaves

See photo pg. 23

■ *Embossing stencils:* Geometric and Romantic.

B1

Embroider the branch and stems using stem stitch.
Draw a single thread from points A. Sew on the beads
and golden leaves.

B1

B2

Pierce the central
holes with the coarse
Erica® piercing tool.
Draw the threads as
indicated. Tape on the
golden leaves.

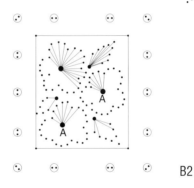

B2

B3

See B2.

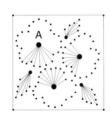

B3

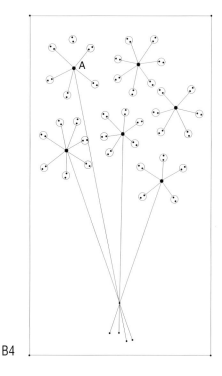

B4
Pull the long threads and the threads going from A. Sew on the beads. Stick on the golden leaves.

B4

B5
Embroider the stems using stem stitch. Leaves: as indicated. Flowers: first draw the long threads to the back, then sew on the beads.

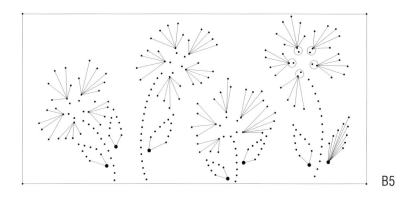

B5

Instructions on pg. 21

Embossed parchment paper

See photo pg. 27

Erica®'s parchment paper is available in white, ivory, light blue, mint and pink. The advantage is that you don't need a light box to emboss it, since the paper is transparent. It is very easy to emboss and used on the outside of a card makes a lovely frame for your embroidery. All four of the embossing stencils are used in this chapter.

C1

Embossing stencil: Decorative. Embroider the three circles as follows: begin with the innermost circle. Insert needle back to front at 1 and draw the thread to 2. Go along the back to 3 and draw the thread to 4, etc., until you have come around 'full circle' and each hole has two threads coming from it. The diameter of the cut-out is 6 cm.

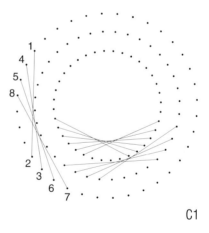

C1

C2

Embossing stencil: Decorative.
Insert needle back to front at 1
and draw the thread to 2. Go
along the back to 3 and draw
the thread to 4, etc., until you
have completed the arch. Do
all the arches in this way, then
pull a straight thread along the
rows of holes. The diameter of
the cut-out is 6.5 cm.

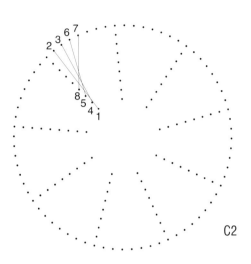

C2

C3

Embossing stencil: Elegant.
Begin with embroidering the
innermost figure: Insert
needle back to front at 1 and
draw the thread to 2. Go
along the back to 3 and draw
the thread to 4, etc. Make the
outside figure in the same
way. The diameter of the cut-
out is 6.5 cm.

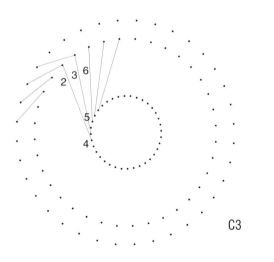

C3

C4

Embossing stencil: Romantic.
Make the holes at A larger with the Erica coarse
piercing tool. Insert needle back to front at A and
draw the threads to the points as indicated. The
cut-out is 3 x 3 cm.

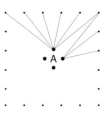

C4

C5

Embroidery: see C4.
The cut-out is 4.8 x 4.8 cm. The cut-
out corners and the embossing
follow the patterns on the
Geometrich embossing stencil.

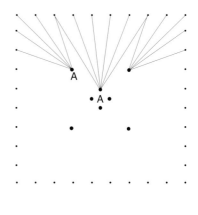

C5

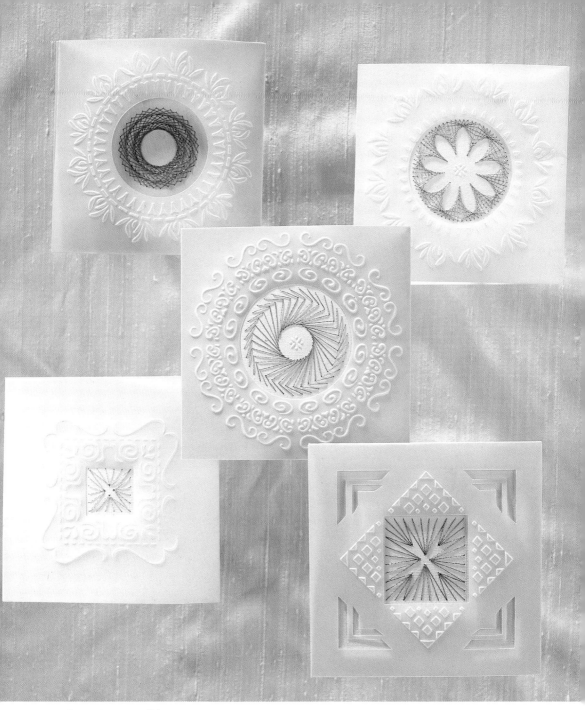

Instructions on pg. 24

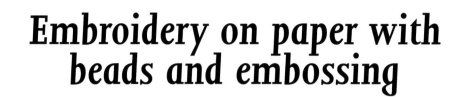

Embroidery on paper with beads and embossing

See photo pg. 31

In this chapter, embroidery patterns are combined with embossing and various beaded borders. Make your own creations!

D1

Insert needle from back to front at all points A and pull threads to the points as indicated. Embroider a bead at all ends (see photo).

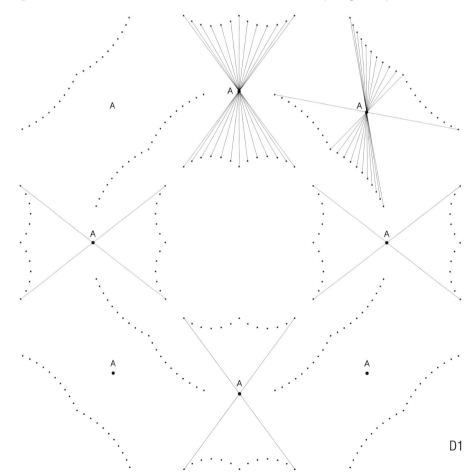

D1

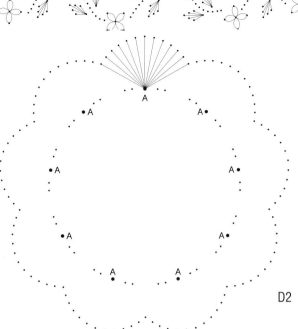

D2

Emboss the border first. Insert needle from back to front at all points A and pull threads as indicated. Embroider the beads in the circle.

D2

D3

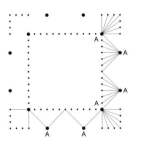

D3

Emboss the edge after piercing. Embroidery: insert needle from back to front at all points A and pull threads to the points as indicated. Embroider a long border with beads around the embossing.

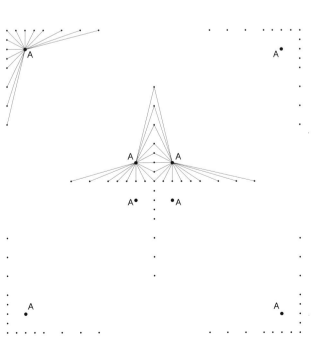

D4

Emboss the borders after piercing. Insert needle from back to front at all points A and pull threads to the points as indicated. Embroider a border with beads.

D4

D5

Emboss the borders after piercing. Insert needle from back to front at all points A and pull threads to the points as indicated Embroider beads in the triangles between the threads.

D5

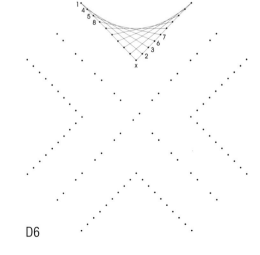

D6

D6

Emboss the borders after piercing. Insert needle back to front at 1 and draw the thread to 2. Go along the back to 3 and draw the thread to 4, etc., until you've finished the corner. Insert needle back to front at X and draw threads along the row of holes. Finish with a pretty beaded border.

Instructions on pg. 28

Grey and pearls

See photo pg. 35

■ Embossing stencil: Geometric

E1

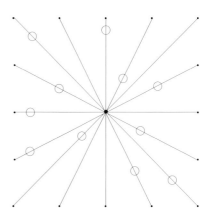

E1

Pierce the central hole larger using Erica®'s coarse piercing tool. Insert the needle back to front through the large hole and draw the threads as indicated, threading a pearl bead onto the thread. The beads are not fastened down and can be moved.

E2

E2

Draw the threads to form the squares, then fasten the beads.

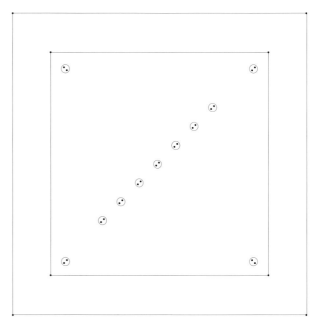

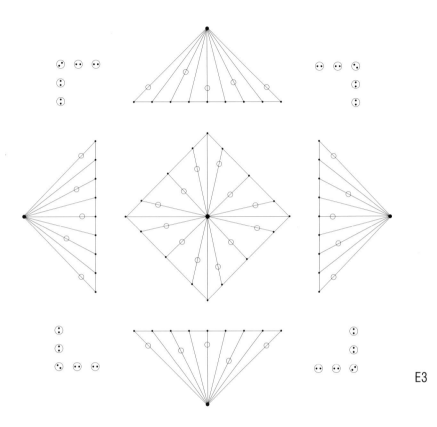

E3

E3

Enlarge the holes where multiple threads will come through, using Erica®'s coarse piercing tool. Insert the needle back to front through the large hole and draw the threads as indicated. Every now and then put a pearl onto your thread.

33

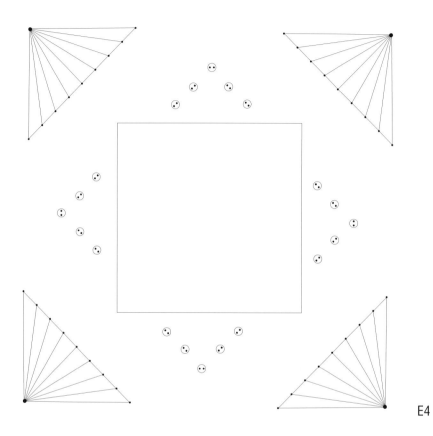

E4

E4
Draw the threads as indicated and fasten the beads where indicated.

Warm yellow with beads

See photo pg. 39

- ■ Embossing stencils: Geometric, Decorative and Romantic.
- ■ Secure the beads where indicated.

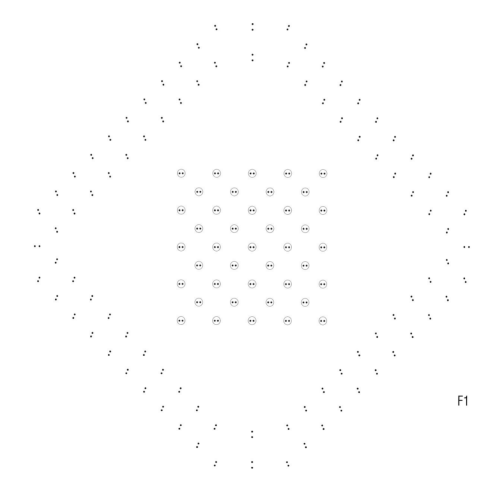

F1

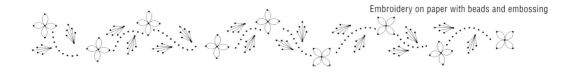

F2

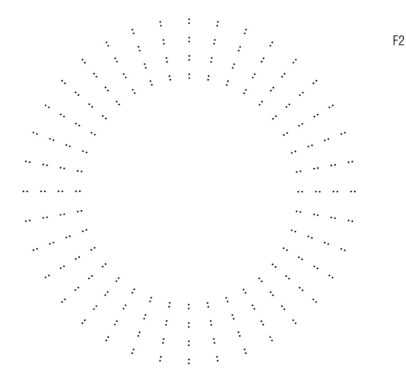

37

38

F3

Instructions on pg. 36

F4

F5

Embossed parchment with cut-outs

See photo pg. 43

The central elements of all four embossing stencils (Geometric, Elegant, Decorative and Romantic) are used in this chapter.

G1

Embossing stencil: Romantic.
Enlarge the holes at A using the Erica coarse piercing tool. Insert needle from back to front at A and draw threads to the points as indicated. The cut-out is 6.5 x 6.5 cm. Draw a thread along the inside edge of the cut-out to finish.

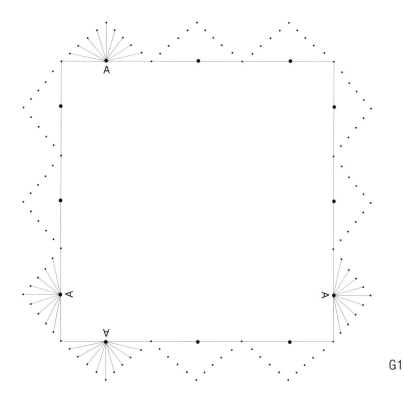

G1

G2

Embossing stencil: Decorative.

Insert needle from back to front at 1 and draw thread to 2. Go along the back to 3 and bring the thread out and to 4, etc, until you have finished the curve. Complete all the curves and draw a straight thread along the rows of holes. The diameter of the cut-out is 7 cm.

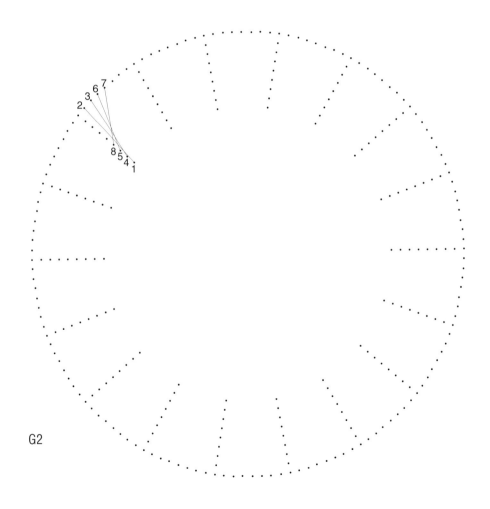

G2

Instructions on pg. 41

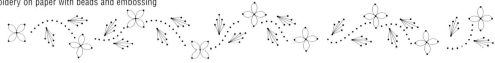

G3

Embossing stencil: Elegant.
Embroidery: see C1.
The diameter of the cut-out is 5 cm.

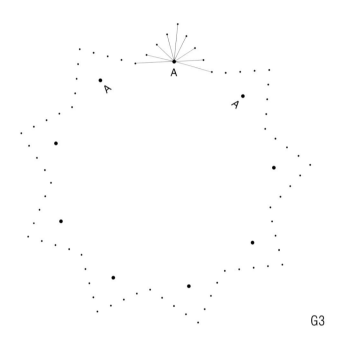

G3

G4

Embossing stencil: Geometric

The cut-out in the card is also made using this stencil. Insert needle from back to front at 1 and draw thread to 2. Go along the back to 3 and bring the thread out and to 4, etc, until you have finished the corner. Draw a straight thread along the rows of holes.

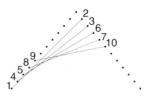

G4

Behind beaded 'bars'

See photo pg. 47

Measure and cut the cut-outs carefully. TIP: Pierce a tiny hole using the extra-fine piercing tool; it will show you precisely where to cut. When stringing beads, try to put on just enough so that no space is left over on the thread. This will depend on the beads you use and their size. Don't pull the thread too tight, or the card may buckle.

I1
The cut-out is 4.5 x 8 cm.

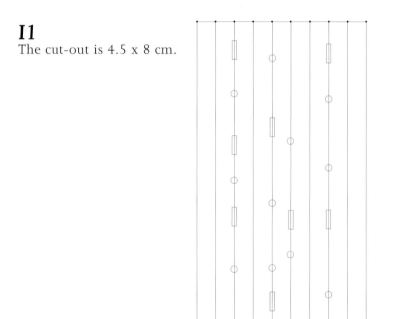

I1

Instructions on pg. 46

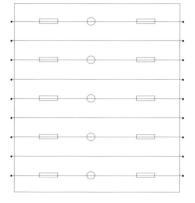

12
The cut-out is 4.5 x 5 cm.

13

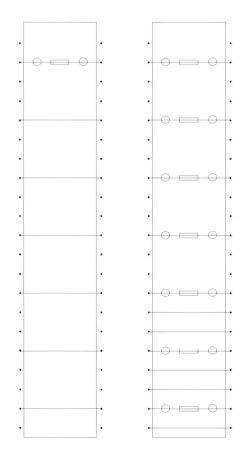

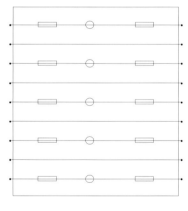

12

13
The cut-outs are 2 x 11 cm.

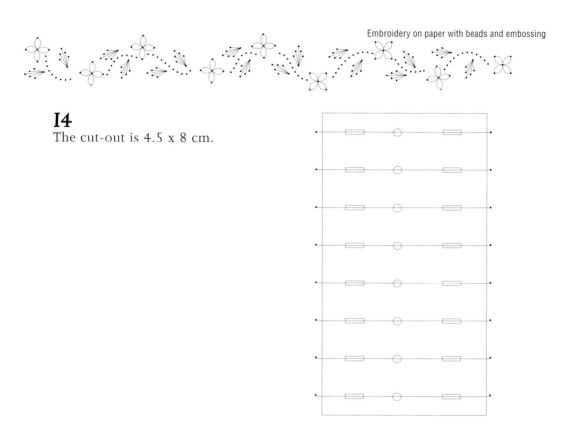

I4
The cut-out is 4.5 x 8 cm.

I4

I5

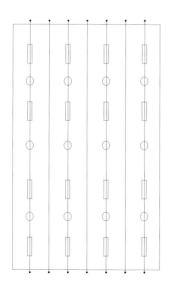

I5
The cut-out is 4 x 6.5 cm.

Embossing with embroidered borders

See photo pg. 51

■ All four embossing stencils are used in this chapter.
■ Finish the cards with shiny blue origami foil.

J1

Embossing stencil: Geometric.
Enlarge the holes where more than one thread will be, using the Erica® coarse piercing tool. Insert needle from back to front though the large hole and draw the threads to the indicated points.

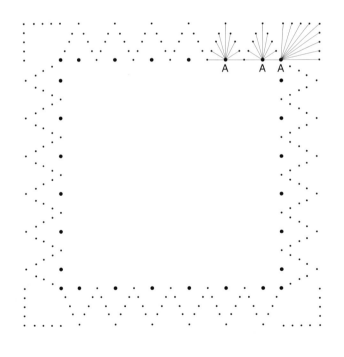

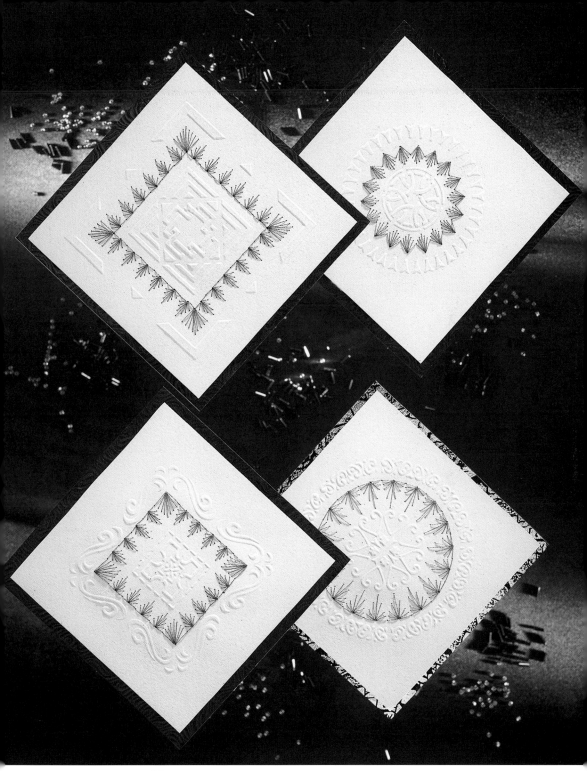

Instructions on pg. 50

J2
Embossing stencil: Romantic.
Embroidery instructions: see J1.

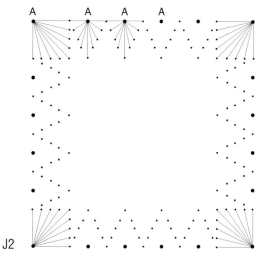

J3
Embossing stencil: Decorative.
Embroidery instructions: see J1.

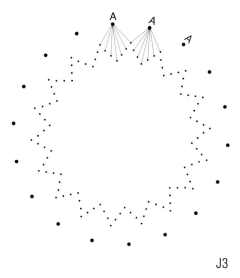

J4
Embossing stencil: Elegant.
Embroidery instructions: see J1.

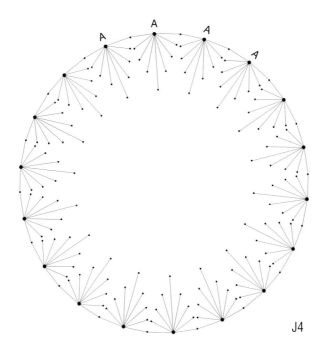

J4

Figures embroidery on paper

Introduction

Real embroidery fans will just love the patterns in this new book:
Figures embroidery on paper. These figures come in all shapes and
colours, sometimes embroidered in three co-ordinated shades of
thread – a feast for the eyes!
Cutting, embossing and embroidery with the new stencils Mandala,
December, Merry Christmas and Circle will put you in the holiday
mood once again!
Something new in this book is framing photos in a frame with an
embroidered edge. Add a bit of embossing, stick them in a book you
or the copy shop made, and you're ready to go.
Have fun!

Erica Fortgens

I am very grateful to Leonie Heuyerjans for her assistance.

Sunny Mandalas

See photo pg. 59

- Use the Mandala stencil to cut and emboss
- Cut the card extra large – 15 × 15 cm!

A1

Pierce the pattern onto the card. Measure between the designs to find the centre line for cutting. Embroider before cutting, and make sure you keep the cellotape close to the embroidery. Insert needle at front at A and pull the thread to the points as indicated.
Finishing: Give some height to the card by using 3D foam. It will also enhance the effect of the cutwork.

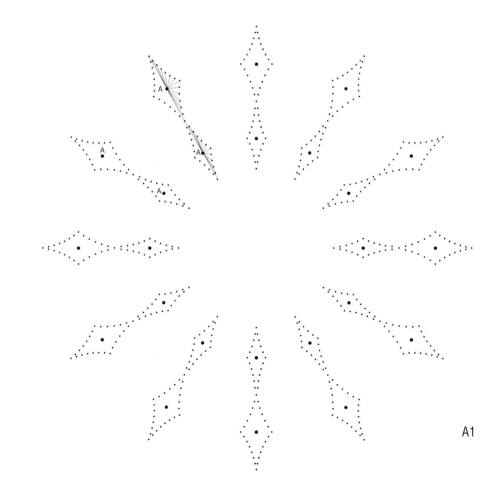

A1

Instructions on pg. 58

A2

Pierce the pattern onto the card and use the ruler to find the centre line between the pierced elements. Emboss here. Emboss before you embroider! Use three different shades of yellow.

Embroidery A: Insert needle at the front at A and draw the thread to the points surrounding it.

Embroidery B: Insert needle at the front at 1 and draw the thread to back at 2. Bring to front at 3 and draw the thread to 4, and so on. Continue until you have a full circle and each hole has two threads coming out of it.

Embroidery C: Insert needle at the front at 1 and draw to 2. Bring to front at 3 and draw thread to 4, etc. until you have a full circle.

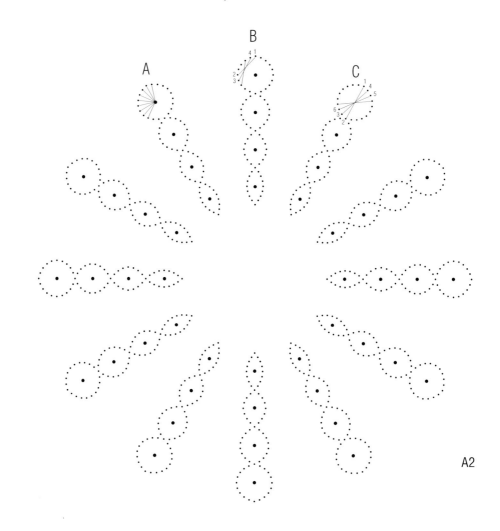

A2

A3

Pierce the pattern onto the card and use the ruler to find the centre line between the pierced elements. Emboss. Embroider with three different shades of yellow.
Insert needle at the front at A and draw threads to the points as indicated. Make sure you pierce the A points with a coarse piercing tool; if you find you need more room while embroidering, open it up a little!

A3

A4

Pierce the pattern onto the card and use the ruler to find the centre line between the pierced elements. Emboss. Embroider with three different shades of yellow.

Use dark yellow (Alcazar metallic) for the innermost threads. Insert needle at front at A and draw threads to the points as indicated.

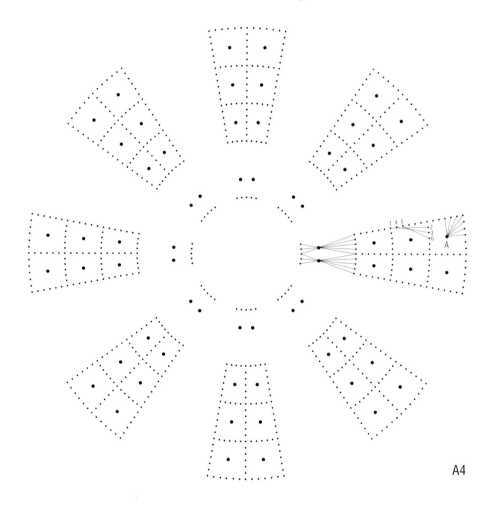

A4

Creations in light blue

See photo pg. 67

■ Embroider on Erica®'s embossing parchment paper
■ *Stencils:* Decorative, Allure and Circle
■ *Under-card:* light blue
■ *Cover:* Erica®'s parchment paper for embossing (light blue)

Important: Parchment paper is transparent, so be careful with the tape you use to fasten the thread at the back. Use a very small piece of tape or make a couple of stitches at the back to attach and tie off threads.

B1

Pierce the pattern onto the card. Emboss using the Decorative stencil. Insert needle at the front at 1 and draw the thread to 2. Go along the back to 3, bring needle to front and draw to 4, etc. until you come back to 1.
Loops: Use the stem stitch and skip three holes.

B1

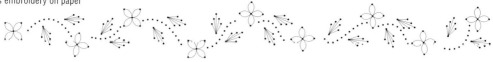

B2

Pierce the pattern onto the card. Emboss using the Decorative stencil.
Embroider the pattern in stem stitch, always skipping three holes.

B2

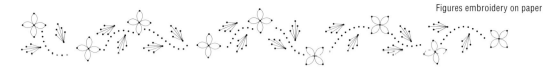

B3

Pierce the pattern onto the card. Emboss using the Circle stencil. Insert needle at front at A and bring thread to the points as indicated.
Loops: Bring back to front at 1 and draw the thread to 2. Go along the back to 3, bring needle to front and draw to 4, etc. until you come back to 1.

B3

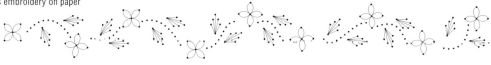

B4

Pierce the pattern onto the card.
Using a circle cutter, cut a 3.4-cm diameter hole in the centre. Emboss the bottom layer with the Decorative stencil.
Emboss the cover card using the Allure stencil. Embroider as follows:
Insert needle at the front at 1 and draw thread to 2. Go along the back to 3 and draw thread to 4, etc., until the curve is done.

B4

Instructions on pg. 63

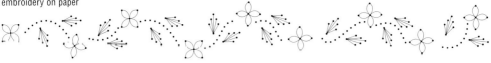

B5

Pierce the pattern onto the card. Emboss using the Circle stencil. Embroider the card as described in B4.

B5

Rosettes

See photo pg. 71

These designs use two shades of salmon-pink thread.

C1
Insert needle at the front at 1 and draw the thread to 2. Go along the back to 3 and draw the thread to 4, etc. until you come back to 1. Make the squares in this way as well.

C1

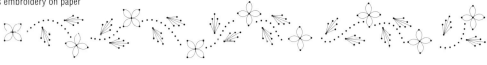

C2

Ovals: Insert needle at the front at 1 and draw the thread to 2. Go along the back to 3 and draw the thread to 4, etc. until there are two threads coming from each hole.

Squares: bring needle back to front at 1 and draw the thread to 2. Go along the back to 3 and draw the thread to 4, etc. until you are back to 1.

C2

Instructions on pg. 69

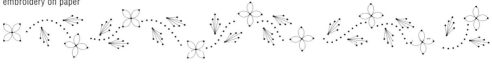

C3

Insert needle at the front at 1 and draw the thread to 2. Go along the
back to 3 and draw the thread to 4, etc. until you are back to 1. Make
the squares in this way as well.

C3

C4

Squares: see instructions under C2.

Intersecting circles: Insert needle at the front at 1 and draw the thread to 2. Go along the back to 3 and draw the thread to 4, etc. until there are two threads coming from each hole.

C4

Radiant stars

See photo pg. 75

- Stencil: December
- If embroidery with metallic thread, use a single strand!

D1

Pierce the pattern onto the card. Use the Ruler to find the central point between the corners, and cut the V shapes out using the stencil December. Embroider the edges as shown at diagram B: Insert needle at the front at 1 and draw the thread to 2. Go along the back to 3 and draw the thread to 4, etc. until the corner is done. Draw a thread along the row of holes.

Instructions on pg. 74

D2

Pierce the pattern onto the card. Use the Ruler to find the position of the cut-out V-shapes. Embroidery: Insert needle at the front at A and draw the threads to the points surrounding it. Other angles: Insert needle at the front at 1 and draw the thread to 2. Go along the back to 3 and draw the thread to 4, etc. until the shape is one. Pull a thread along the row of holes.

D2

D3

Emboss the stars after you pierce the pattern. For the angles, see D2.

D3

D4

Pierce the pattern onto the card.
Emboss the candle design in the outside corners. Use the Ruler to find
the centre between the two pierced corners. Mark with pencil and cut
out the angles using the December stencil. Embroider the card as
described in D2.

D4

Instructions on pg. 80

Pretty in pink

See photo pg.79

The embossing is done using the Erica® Ruler and Circle stencil.

E1

Pierce the pattern onto the card. Emboss using the Ruler for the flowers and Circle stencil for the centre.
Embroidery:
Insert needle at the front at 1 and draw the thread to 2. Go along the back to 3 and draw the thread to 4, etc. until the curl is done.

E1

E2

See E1.

E2

E3
See E1.
Hearts: The heart pattern is
in the Circle stencil.

E3

E4
See E1.

E4

Floral designs in pastel green

See photo pg. 83

- ■ *Stencils*: Mandala and Circle.
- ■ Use two shades of pastel green that go together.

F1

Insert needle at the front at 1 and draw the thread to 2. Go along the back to 3 and draw the thread to 4, etc. until you come back to 1. *Curves*: embroider with stem stitch, skipping three holes for a heavier effect.

F1

Instructions on pg. 82

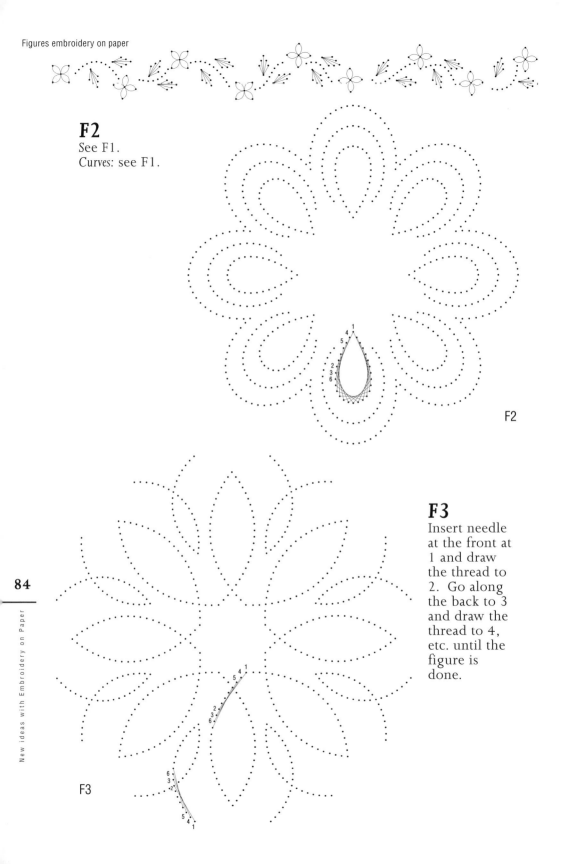

F2
See F1.
Curves: see F1.

F2

F3
Insert needle
at the front at
1 and draw
the thread to
2. Go along
the back to 3
and draw the
thread to 4,
etc. until the
figure is
done.

84

F3

F4

See F3.

F4

Circles in purple

See photo pg. 87

■ Stencils: Circle and Mandala.
■ Use three shades of purple and lilac thread that go together.

G1

Insert needle at the front at A and draw the thread to the points as indicated.

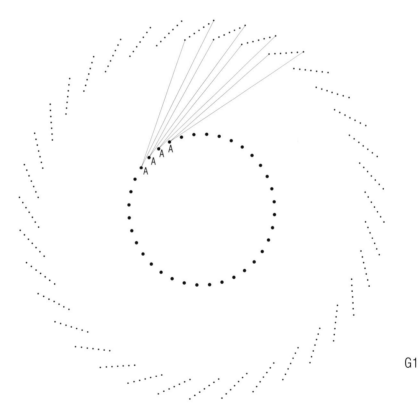

G1

Instructions on pg. 86

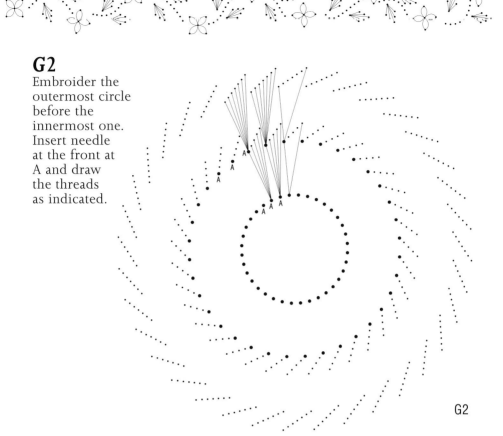

G2

Embroider the
outermost circle
before the
innermost one.
Insert needle
at the front at
A and draw
the threads
as indicated.

G2

G3

Take a double piece of lilac card stock.
Using the Circle stencil, cut the round
cut-out out of the card. Cut the triangles
outside the circle. Emboss the border.
Glue a dark purple card, with the same
sized hole cut from its centre, behind the
top card. Cut the triangles in the bottom
card and embroider the pattern in it.
Insert needle at the front at A and draw
the threads to all the surrounding points.

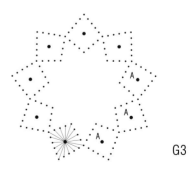

G3

Elegant in aqua

See photo pg. 91

- Stencils: Mandala, Elegant and Erica®'s Ruler.
- Use a single strand when embroidering with metallic thread.

For all patterns, embroider using stem stitch. For a heavier effect, skip three holes. Use the borders on Erica®'s Ruler for the embossing in and around the figures.

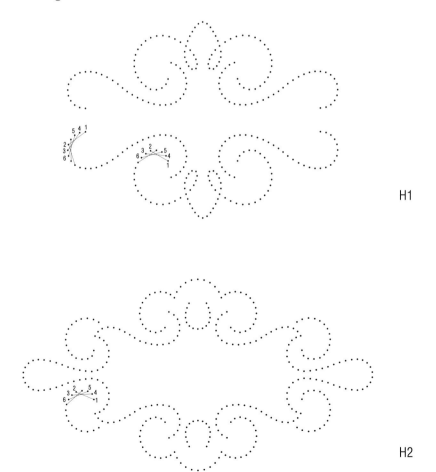

H1

H2

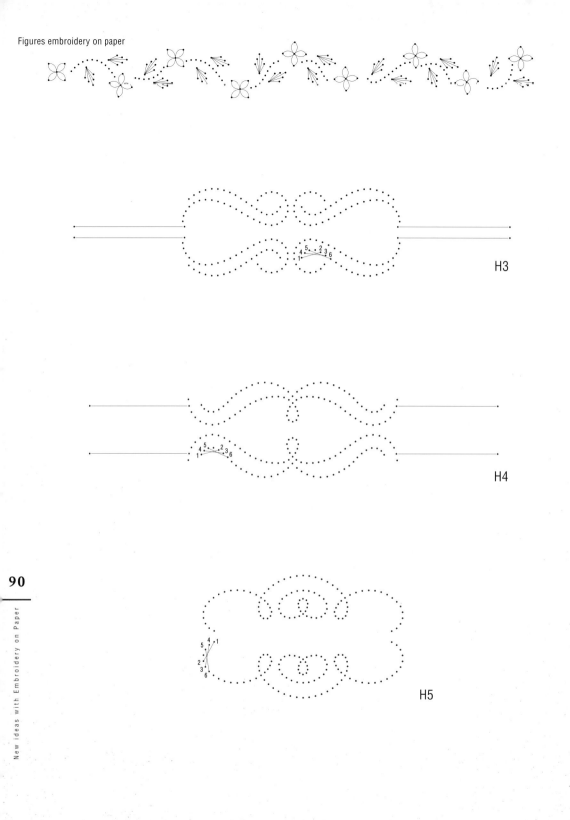

H3

H4

H5

Instructions on pg. 89

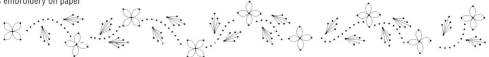

Photos to frame and take away

See photo pg. 95

Add an extra dimension to the way you present your latest photos! Cut them out, glue a contrasting piece of paper behind them and put them in a frame you embroidered yourself! Add a bit of embossed corner or a border as a finishing touch, and your presentation is complete. And what do you think of this next idea: take the whole thing to the copy shop where in the wink of an eye your cards can be made into a booklet -ready to go!

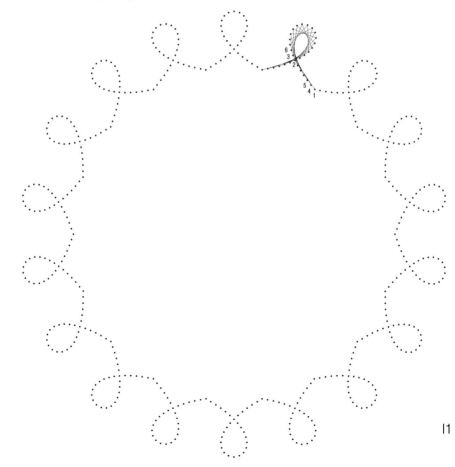

Stencils used: Decorative, Mandala and Circle.

I1

Insert needle at the front at 1 and draw the thread to 2. Go behind to 3 and draw the thread to 4, etc. until the loop is finished. Make the following loop.

I2

Insert needle at the front at A and draw the threads to the points surrounding. Using different colours (see the photo) gives it a cheerful look!

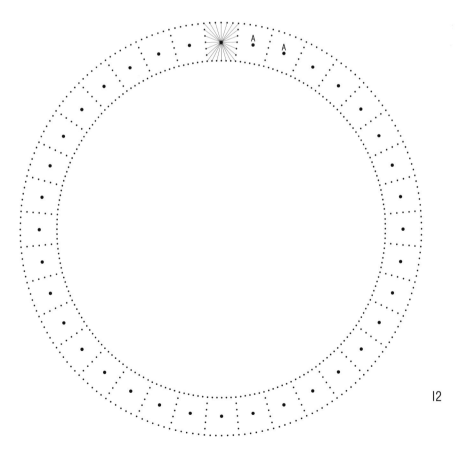

I2

I3

Insert needle at the front at 1 and draw the thread to 2. Go along the back to 3 and draw the thread to 4, etc. until the triangle is finished.

I3

Instructions on pg. 92

14

For both A and B, insert needle at the front at 1 and draw the thread to 2. Go along the back to 3 and draw the thread to 4, etc. until you are back at 1.

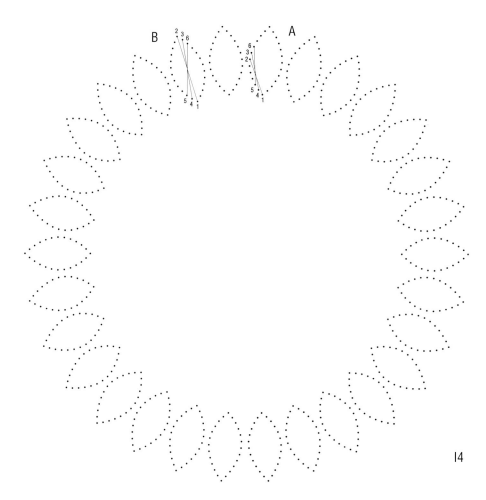

14

Patchwork greeting cards with embroidery on paper

Introduction

I've used several different techniques. Some of the blocks are cut to form a cut-out, with a lovely new paper underneath: Paperpatch paper. Used in strips or in combinations of colours, it gives a gorgeous effect. Also important; put tiny bits of foam tape on the card, then stick it onto the piece of Paperpatch, any piece you like.

Besides cutting cut-outs, embossing is always a nice way to fill the empty spaces – indulge yourself!

The success of the L'ouvre cards has inspired the newest additions to the line, the L'ouvre frames. They consist of various elements: inner and outer frames, corners and ornaments. Just cut them out with a sharp hobby knife. Use the elements in combination with each other or set them apart. There are many, many possibilities, for the other techniques as well.

Erica Fortgens

I am very grateful to Leonie Heuyerjans, as well as to Anneke Kaufman for her collaboration.

Paperpatch paper

See photo pg. 102

Once you have cut out the corners of the patchwork stencils, you can use the lovely Paperpatch paper. You can alternate and combine strips of various colours; just look at the photos!
Four different packages are available, each with six different A5 sheets, in Arte, Rose, Bloc and Gold.

L'ouvre frames

In the last chapters of this book we use the L'ouvre frames for your creations. Most of them consist of several elements, for example, a frame with a smaller frame inside or corners with ornaments inside them. Cut the elements apart on a cutting mat, using a hobby knife. If you're not using embroidery, the ornament can be hung by a thread in the large frame. Then tape this frame down with a few tiny pieces of foam tape; it adds depth and allows you to see through the piece since the lasered part is transparent. You can use these frames to embellish any and every creation you make, including those using other techniques. Enjoy yourself!
The L'ouvre frames used in this book are intended for framing embroidered, cut and embossed patchwork blocks. Use tiny pieces of foam tape to mount them; then you can peer through the gossamer veils! It is also nice to use a cream-coloured frame for a darker card.

Finishing

For finishing your cards I recommend using very small pieces of foam tape or 3D kit to give more depth. It's a nice effect, especially combined with the Paperpatch paper and the L'ouvre frames.

100

Green/blue Paperpatch

See photo pg. 138

Materials needed

■ Stencil: patchwork 1A
■ Paperpatch: Bloc
■ Thread: Floss

Draw the thread all the way through the needle until you have a double thread.

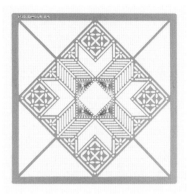

1. First pierce the pattern through the card, then cut the openings from the card. Emboss. Embroider the triangles as follows: Insert needle at the front at 1 and draw the thread to 2. Go along the back to 3 and draw the thread to 4, etc. until you are all the way around the triangle. Complete all the triangles this way. Tape narrow strips of solid green paper round the patchwork block. Tape the decorated paper behind it.

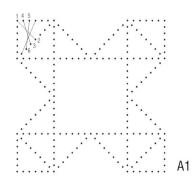

A1

Arte

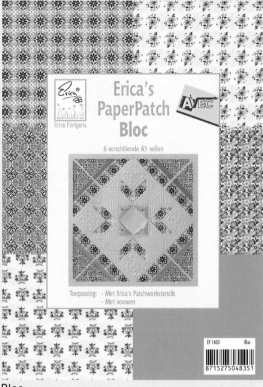

Bloc

Gold

Rose

L'ouvre frames, corners and ornaments

2. Insert needle at the front at A and draw the thread to the points indicated. Paperpatch: work with strips, alternating solid green and the paper with fruit baskets.

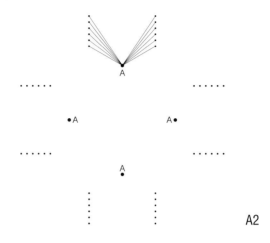

A2

3. Insert needle at the front at A (pierce these holes very large). Draw the threads from A to the surrounding points as indicated. Tape strips of Paperpatch behind the block and fill the triangle with decorated paper.

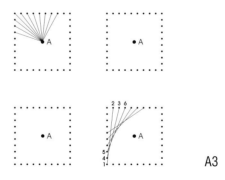

A3

4. After piercing, cut the cut-out. Insert needle at the front at A and draw the threads to the surrounding points as indicated. Tape the fruit-basket paper behind the small openings, and fill the corners with contrasting Paperpatch.

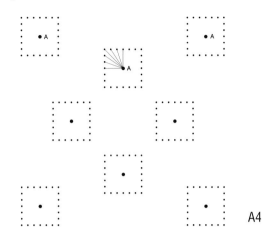

A4

TIP
Take a L'ouvre border that can be used for weaving (you'll see small slits in them). Weave ribbon, paper strips, wool or raffia through the border. Use it as a decoration next to the border embroidered using the pattern at the top of the page!

Golden Star

See photo pg. 107

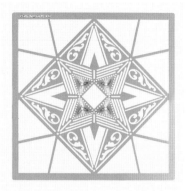

Materials needed
- Stencil: patchwork 1B
- Paperpatch: Gold
- Yarn: Anchor Alcazar metallic gold

Always use a single strand when using metallic thread.

1. After piercing, cut the cut-out. Embroidery: Insert needle at the front at A and from A draw the threads to the points indicated. Use three different kinds of Paperpatch to finish the openings in the cut-out.

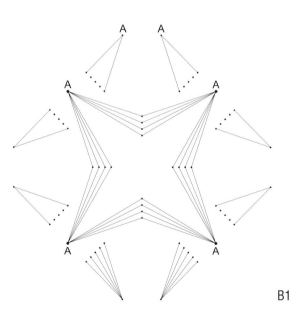

B1

Instructions on pg. 106

2. After piercing, cut the cut-out. Emboss the stripes of the star. Insert needle at the front at A and draw the threads as indicated. Use two different kinds of Paperpatch to finish the card.

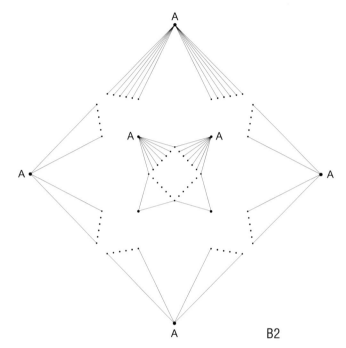

B2

3. After piercing and cutting, emboss. Embroidery:
Insert needle at the front at A and draw the threads to the points indicated. Paperpatch: first stick the strips along the block and fill the rest of the corner with contrasting paper.

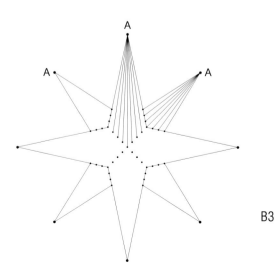

B3

4. After piercing and cutting, emboss. Embroider the star as follows: Insert needle at the front at A and draw the threads to the points indicated. Stick a single piece of Paperpatch behind the cut-out.

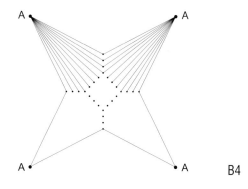

A   A

A   A   B4

TIP
Use very thin strips of foam tape or drops of 3D foam on the back of the card along the cut-out.
Lay the Paperpatch paper on the table in front of you. Hold the card over the paper; this way you can choose the piece you want to use. Stick the card on top of it, and trim the excess paper away.

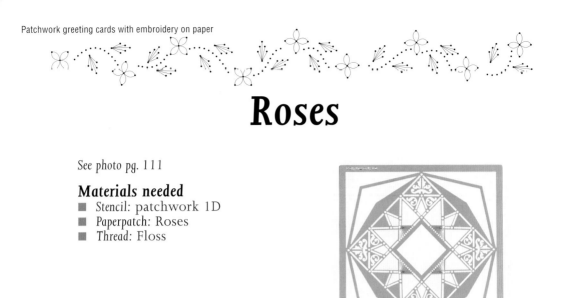

Roses

See photo pg. 111

Materials needed
- Stencil: patchwork 1D
- Paperpatch: Roses
- Thread: Floss

1. Cut the cut-out from the card. Pierce the pattern. Do the embossing. Embroider the crosses as follows: Insert needle at the front at 1 and draw the thread to 2. Go along the back to 3 and draw the thread to 4, etc., until you have finished the cross. Place the card, raised with foam tape, onto the Paperpatch, using two different kinds of paper.

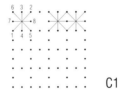

C1

TIP
Instead of cutting one of the cut-outs in this chapter, you can pick out a L'ouvre frame. Drip 3D foam along the frame and glue it onto your creation!

Instructions on pg. 110

2. Using a pencil and ruler, draw an X at the centre of the card. Fit the corner of the stencil in a corner of the X and cut the cut-out in the card; the corners of the stencil form a central figure this way. Embroidery: Insert needle at the front at A and draw the threads to the points indicated. Paperpatch: take four different pieces of the same paper and place the roses at the centre.

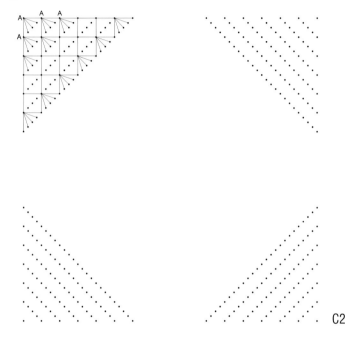

C2

112

TIP
You can alter the pattern yourself: Use pencil and ruler to draw an X on a piece of white paper: this is your new home-made piercing pattern. Cut out the four corners of the embroidery pattern and place them at the corners of the X; you'll embroider a rectangle this way. You can frame it with a cut-out, an embossing border or a L'ouvre frame.

3. Cut, pierce and emboss the card. Embroidery: Insert needle at the front through the large hole A and draw the threads to the points indicated.
Important: cut the large holes very large, since you're using a double thread. Apply a small Paperpatch rose and use contrasting paper for the cut-out.

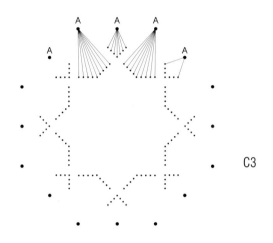

C3

4. Cut, pierce and emboss the card. Embroider as follows: Insert needle at the front at A and draw the threads to the points indicated. Apply a Paperpatch rose bouquet and use the green paper for the corners.

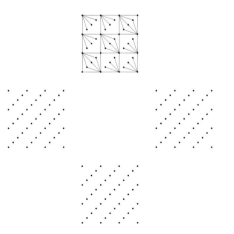

C4

Composition in blue

See photo pg. 115

Materials needed
- Stencil: patchwork 1C
- Paperpatch: Arte
- Thread: Floss

1. Cut, pierce and emboss the card. Embroider the centre: Insert needle at the front at large hole and draw the threads to the surrounding points. Now insert needle at the front at A and draw the threads to the points indicated. Frame with a single strand of gold metallic thread. Finishing: use four pieces from the same sheet of Paperpatch.

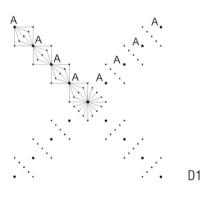

D1

Instructions on pg. 114

2. Cut, pierce and emboss the card. Embroidery: Insert needle at the front at 1 and draw the thread to 2. Go along the back to 3 and draw the thread to 4, etc., until you have finished the cross. Do all the crosses in this way. Apply Paperpatch as shown in the photo.

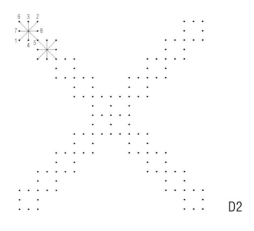

D2

3. This card is not embroidered; there is no pierced pattern. Make an X on the card with a pencil and ruler to mark the centre point. Shift the corner of the stencil until it fits in the corner of the X. Cut the triangle and the first border out. Repeat for all corners. Now place the stencil on the card and cut out the corners. Emboss the wide border as shown in the photo. Use three different Paperpatch sheets for the background.

4. Cut, pierce and emboss the card. Embroidery: Make sure the large holes are pierced quite large. Insert needle at the front at A and B and draw the threads to the points indicated. Apply Paperpatch as shown in the photo.

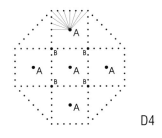

D4

117

TIP
A variation these cards is to frame it with a L'ouvre frame, using very small pieces of foam tape or 3D foam.

Patchwork in green

See photo pg. 119

Materials needed
- Stencil: patchwork 2
- Paperpatch: Bloc
- Thread: Floss

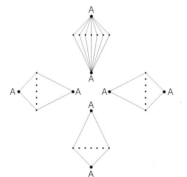

1. Pierce the pattern through the card. Do the embossing; this will show how the card is divided. Cut the elements from the card. Embroidery: Insert needle at the front at A and draw the threads to the points indicated. Apply Paperpatch paper raised with foam tape.

118

E1

TIP
An idea for the border at the top of this page: take a rectangular card, embroider the border and work the L'ouvre corners on the left and right of the border to frame it.

Instructions on pg. 118

2. Pierce the pattern through the card. Do the embossing using the central area of the patchwork 2 stencil. Embroidery of the central area: Insert needle at the front at A and draw the threads to the surrounding points. Use a lighter shade of floss and a double thread. Outer areas: Insert needle at the front at 1 and draw the thread to 2. Go along the back to 3 and draw the thread to 4, etc., until you have finished the square.

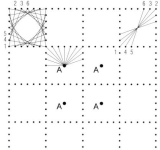

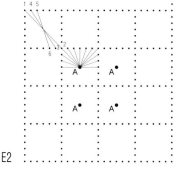

E2

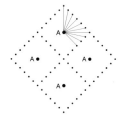

E3

3. Pierce the pattern through the card. Do the embossing. Cut the cut-outs out. Embroidery: Insert needle at the front at A and draw the threads to the points indicated. Apply the Paperpatch paper, raised a little with foam tape.

4. Pierce the pattern through the card. Do the embossing. Cut the openings in the card. Embroidery: Insert needle at the front at A and draw the threads to the surrounding points. Insert needle at the front at B and draw the threads to the points indicated. Apply Paperpatch paper with foam tape.

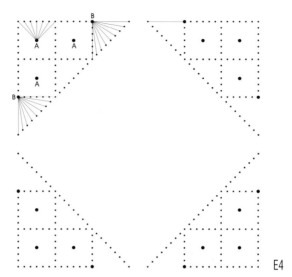

E4

121

TIP
You can use these embroidered corners in other ways: draw an X on a sheet of white paper using a pencil and ruler: this will be your new embroidery piercing pattern. Fit the corners of the piercing pattern in here, with points toward the centre at, say, 0.5 or 1 cm from each other. This will give you a completely different piercing pattern, that you can frame with an embossing border or L'ouvre frame.

You can also hang or glue a L'ouvre ornament in the centre of the above piercing pattern.

Patchwork with embossing

See photo pg. 123

Materials needed

- ■ *Stencil*: patchwork 1D
- ■ *L'ouvre frame*: these cards are all finished with a L'ouvre frame. Use a few very small pieces of foam tape to raise the frame a bit. It makes a beautiful effect!
- ■ *Thread*: Alcazar, two shades of pastel green

1. Embroider the crosses as follows: Insert needle at the front at 1 and draw the thread to 2. Go along the back to 3 and draw the thread to 4, etc., until you are all the way around the cross. Insert needle at the front at all points A and from A draw the threads to the points indicated.

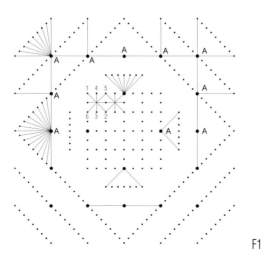

F1

Instructions on pg. 122

2. Pierce the pattern through the card. Emboss the indicated points. Embroidery: Insert needle at the front at A and draw the threads to the surrounding points. Do all triangles and rectangles this way. Frame the elements with a single strand of gold thread.

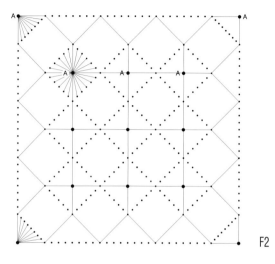

F2

3. Pierce the pattern through the card. Do the embossing. Embroidery: Insert needle at the front at A and draw the threads to the points indicated. Frame the elements with a single strand of gold thread.

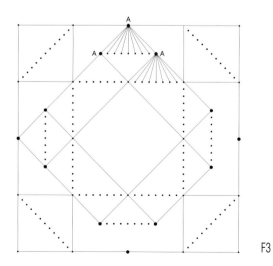

F3

4. Pierce the pattern through the card. Do the embossing. Embroidery: Insert needle at the front at 1 and draw the thread to 2. Go along the back to 3 and draw the thread to 4, etc., until you finish the triangle. Do all the triangles in this way. Frame the elements with a single strand of gold thread.

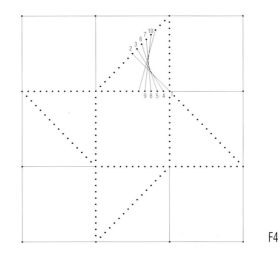

F4

TIP
A fun way to use the border design at the top of this page: Take a rectangular card, embroider the border vertically, and frame the embroidered border on both sides with a L'ouvre frame.

TIP
Here's another way to make your own creation with the embroidery border at the top of this page:
Take 5 cm of the piercing pattern as an embroidery design. Using pencil and ruler, draw a 5.5 cm square. Put the embroidery border on the four sides of the square along the outer edge. This gives you a square border to embroider. Glue an ornament from the L'ouvre collection inside it.

Patchwork with L'ouvre

See photo pg. 127

Materials needed
- Stencil: patchwork 1C and 1B
- L'ouvre frames, raised with pieces of foam tape
- Thread: Alcazar in three shades of yellow

Patchwork 1C

Patchwork 1B

1. Pierce the pattern through the card. Do the embossing with patchwork stencil 1B. Embroider the card as follows: Insert needle at the front at all points A and draw the threads to the points indicated. Insert needle at the front at all points B and draw the threads to the points indicated. Draw all other threads in gold as indicated.

126

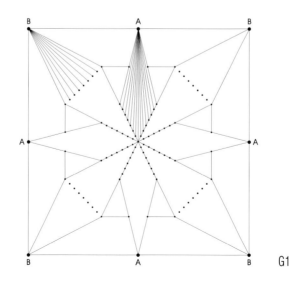

G1

Instructions on pg. 126

2. Pierce the pattern through the card. Note: the four triangles in the centre come from patchwork stencil 1B. Do the striped embossing using patchwork stencil 1C. Embroidery: Insert needle at all points A and draw the threads to the points indicated.

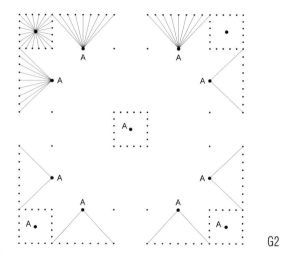

G2

3. Pierce the pattern through the card. Do the embossing. Embroidery: Insert needle at the front at all points A and draw the threads to the points indicated. Rectangles: Insert needle at the front at 1 and draw the thread to 2. Go along the back to 3 and draw the thread to 4, etc., until you have finished the rectangle. Draw all other threads in gold.

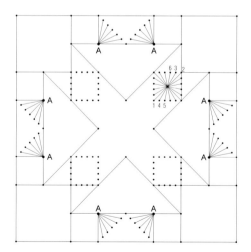

G3

4. Pierce the pattern through the card. Do the embossing. Embroider the triangles in three shades of yellow that go well with each other. Insert needle at the front at 1 and draw the thread to 2. Go along the back to 3 and draw the thread to 4, etc., until you have finished the triangle. Frame the triangles with a single gold thread and the rectangle with a gold thread.

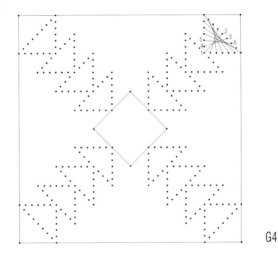

G4

TIP G2
Yet another variation: skip the embroidered and embossed elements from the centre, and use 3D foam to glue a L'ouvre ornament inside it.

TIP G4
As a variation on this pattern, you can skip the frame and embossing. Instead glue L'ouvre corners between the embroidered elements (using 3D foam) – it will make a completely different card.

L'ouvre

See photo pg. 131

Materials needed

- Stencil: patchwork 1D, patchwork 2, patchwork 1C
- L'ouvre frames, raised with small pieces of foam tape
- Thread: Floss and Alcazar gold metallic

Patchwork 1D

Patchwork 2

Patchwork 1C

1. Pierce the pattern through the card. Do the embossing. Embroidery: Insert needle at the front at 1 and draw the thread to 2. Go along the back to 3 and draw the thread to 4, etc., until you have finished the triangle. Frame the elements with a single gold thread. Frame the patchwork block with a gold thread.

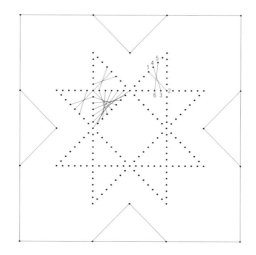

H1

Instructions on pg. 130

2. Pierce the pattern through the card. Using a pencil, draw lines on the back side of the card from hole to hole so you can see the divisions. The embossing for this figure is done as shown on the photo. Embroidery: Insert needle at the front at A and draw the threads to the points indicated. Draw all gold threads.

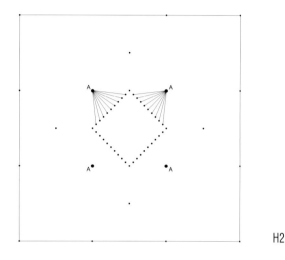

H2

3. Pierce the pattern through the card. Do the embossing. Embroidery: Insert needle at the front at 1 and draw the thread to 2. Go along the back to 3 and draw the thread to 4, etc., until the figure is finished. Repeat on the other side. Corners: Insert needle at the front at A and draw the threads to the points indicated.

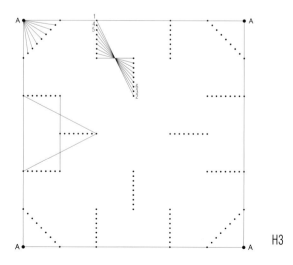

H3

4. Pierce the pattern through the card. Using a pencil and ruler, draw on the back side of the card two X's (one diagonally over the other) to determine the centre. Use this to emboss the hearts with patchwork stencil 2. Embroidery: Insert needle at the front at 1 and draw the thread to 2. Go along the back to 3 and draw the thread to 4, etc., until you have finished the triangle. .

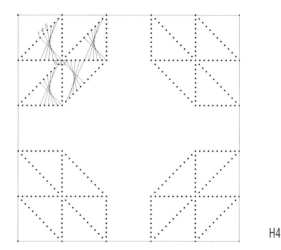

H4

Composition in gold

See photo pg. 135

Materials needed

- Stencil: patchwork 2, patchwork 1B, patchwork 1C
- Card stock: Gold 250 gr.
- Thread: Alcazar metallic gold
- L'ouvre frames, raised with small pieces of foam tape

Patchwork 1C

Patchwork 2

Patchwork 1D

1. Pierce the pattern through the card. Do the embossing. Embroider the crosses as follows: Insert needle at the front at 1 and draw the thread to 2. Go along the back to 3 and draw the thread to 4, etc., until you have finished the cross.

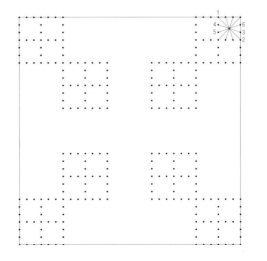

I1

Instructions on pg. 134

2. Pierce the pattern through the card. Do the embossing. Embroider the cross shapes as follows: Insert needle at the front at 1 and draw the thread to 2. Go along the back to 3 and draw the thread to 4, etc., until you have finished the cross.

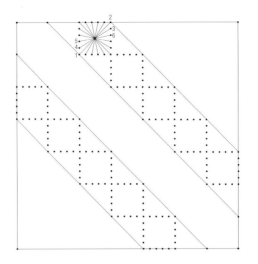

12

3. See card no. 2.

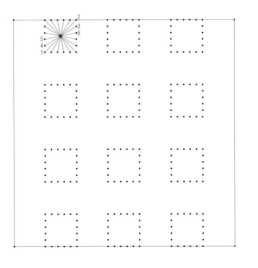

13

136

4. Pierce the pattern through the card. Do the embossing. Insert needle at the front at all points A and draw the threads to the points indicated.

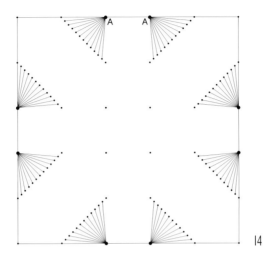

I4

137

TIP I2
As a variation on this pattern, instead of the L'ouvre frame, you can use 3D foam to stick L'ouvre corners in the upper right and lower left corners of the block.

Instructions on pg. 101

More available books with Embroidery
on paper, see next pages.

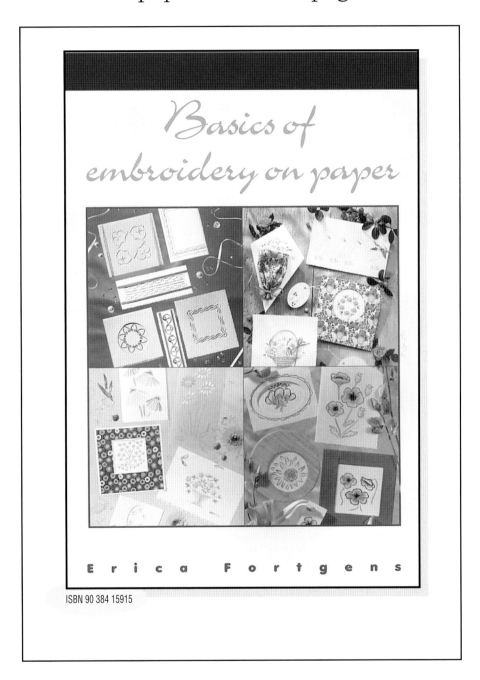

Basics of
embroidery on paper

E r i c a   F o r t g e n s

ISBN 90 384 15915

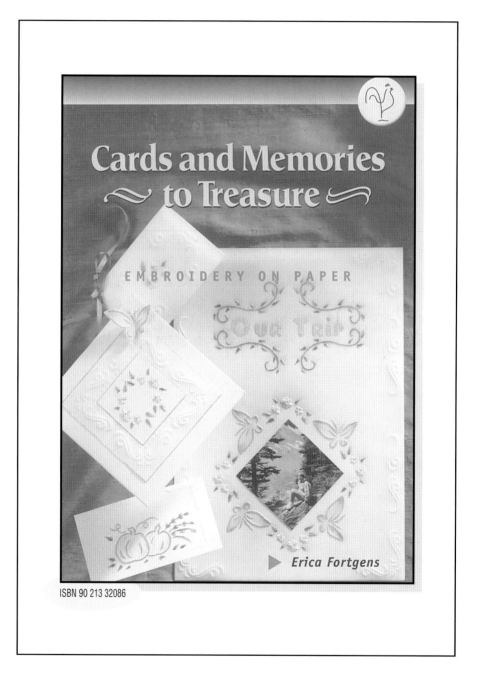

EMBROIDERY ON PAPER

Cards and Memories
to Treasure

Erica Fortgens

ISBN 90 213 32086

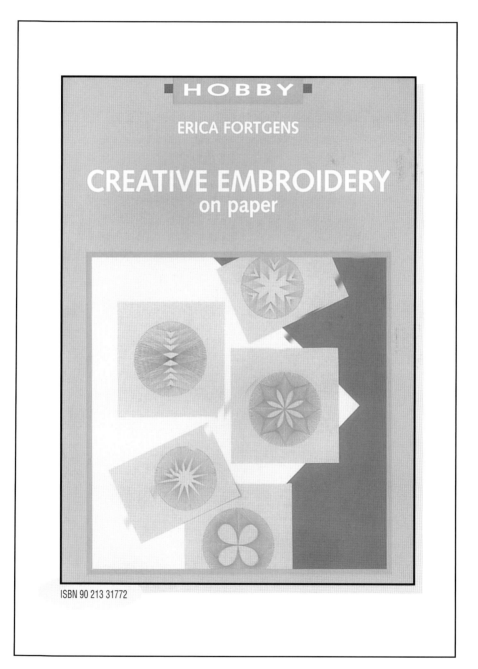

HOBBY

ERICA FORTGENS

CREATIVE EMBROIDERY
on paper

ISBN 90 213 31772

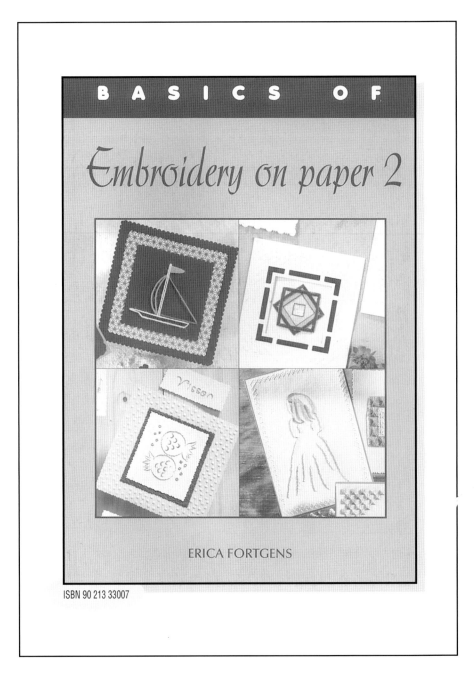

BASICS OF

Embroidery on paper 2

ERICA FORTGENS

ISBN 90 213 33007

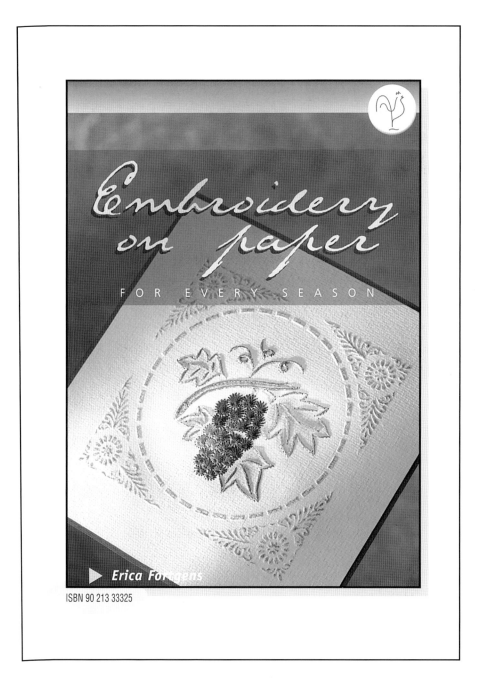

Embroidery on paper

FOR EVERY SEASON

► *Erica Fortgens*

ISBN 90 213 33325

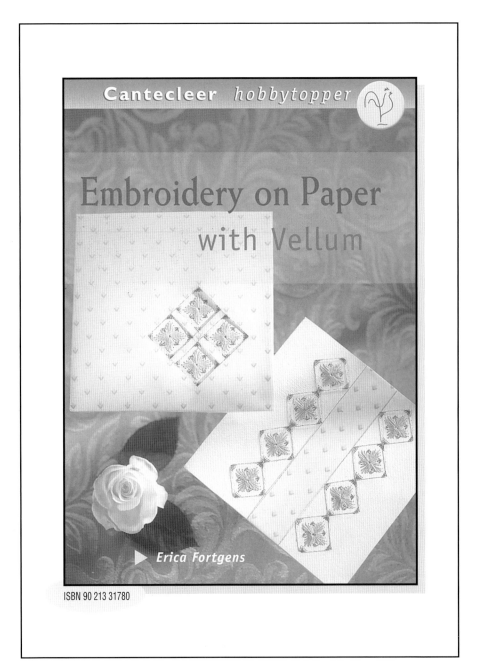

Cantecleer *hobbytopper*

Embroidery on Paper
with Vellum

▶ *Erica Fortgens*

ISBN 90 213 31780